sawada coffee style

Hiroshi Sawada

INTRODUCTION

In April 2010, I opened the doors to my first coffee shop, STREAMER COFFEE COMPANY in Shibuya, Tokyo. At that time, the majority of the coffee shops existing in Japan mainly belonged to one of four styles; traditional Japanese-tearoom known as "kissaten", Italian type "bar", or, Seattle and Japanese mainstream chain-stores, none of which were anything like the independent coffee shops I grew to know in Seattle.

By definition, a Seattle style independent coffee shop typically competes by distinguishing itself from local major chain-stores by providing services and products that require technical skills such as performing latte art, home roasting coffee beans and quite often, baristas are not required to wear a uniform or apron like the mega shops.

I wanted people in Japan to be able to experience this Seattle style independent coffee shop without flying all the way to the US, thus my decision was made to open STREAMER COFFEE COMPANY.

For the interior, I decided to implement an industrial design by placing authentic American factory style chairs in an area of "undressed" reinforced concrete, which, I believe was a novel design at the time in the industry. In fact, upon seeing the interior with steel bars exposed from the concrete walls and ceiling, a person who walked his dog and passed by my shop everyday asked me when the construction will be over, after having opened the shop a few days earlier!

In keeping with my wish to faithfully revive details of an independent Seattle style coffee shop, customers were required to ask staff for the key to the toilet in order to use it. Many Japanese customers were unhappy with this rule, but a number of those who were familiar with this Seattle style custom enjoyed the minute details.

Until then, the majority of independent coffee shops in Japan also offered food during lunch hours, however, unlike the others, I only served a limited option of espresso and doughnuts which caused customers to ask, "is this the only menu you have?".

Japan is the one and only country in the world where one is able to buy coffee anywhere at a low price, be it from the unbelievable number of vending machines or convenient stores. This meant that many independent coffee shops had difficulty in making ends meet simply from coffee sales revenue and were left with the option of either gaining sales revenue per customer by serving food or hiking up the price of coffee by providing full customer service. My question at the time was how I would succeed in opening and maintaining a Seattle style self-service coffee shop selling only coffee in Shibuya where the rent is not cheap.

I wanted to change the general perception of coffee prices in Japan, namely that full-serviced coffee is expensive while self-serviced coffee is cheap. My wish was to provide top quality coffee even as a self-serviced takeout. In order to do so, I decided upon an open-kitchen layout where the customer can enjoy watching me perform latte art in front of them, and in doing so, provide the extra incentive equal to or beyond a cup of coffee at a full-serviced shop. This was inspired from my visits to traditional Japanese sushi and tempura restaurants. Eating at a counter seat of a sushi or tempura restaurant does not come cheap. Quite the opposite, it is expensive. But I perceived the counter seat as a front row viewing of live art!

Up until then, typically, the shop staff would place a lid on take out coffee for safety purposes but I decided that I would give a live performance of latte art in a paper cup and have the customer place the lid after enjoying the artwork.

Amidst the times when everyone was required to wear a uniform in Japanese coffee shops, I established my personal "barista fashion" of serving coffee wearing a Supreme beanie cap, t-shirt and shorts. I thrive in the challenge of always doing what no one has ever done before.

As Japan started to slowly recover from the effects of the Great East Japan Earthquake in 2011, there was a rush of new independent style coffee shops opening in Tokyo and now, the majority of the shops follow my style. It is now common to see latte art performed in paper cups and baristas serving coffee in shirts without collars. At the same time, Japanese customers also spend more on coffee than before.

In December 2015, six years after opening my first shop in Tokyo, I opened the doors to sawada coffee in Chicago, Illinois. This is a monumental step forward from being the one and only shop in Japan to the one and only shop in the world.

I opened "sawada coffee" implementing my current ideas and concepts together with the lessons learned from my previous experiences, be they good or bad. I sincerely hope that my book, which explains my thoughts behind the concept and actual business operations will be a source of reference or help to those who are planning to open their own shop, or already own a shop.

Sawada Hiroshi

2010年4月、私は東京の渋谷にストリーマーコーヒーカンパニーというカフェをオープンしました。当時、日本では、喫茶店・イタリア系バール・シアトル系や日本のコーヒーチェーン店というのが代表的なカフェで、私がシアトルで体験したようなインディペンデント系カフェ（独立系カフェ）が存在していませんでした。

　シアトルのインディペンデント系カフェとは、シアトル系大手コーヒーショップに対抗するコーヒーショップで、バリスタはエプロンなどの制服に縛られることなく、ラテアートや店内で自家焙煎したり、大手コーヒーチェーン店ができない技術でグルメコーヒーをセルフサービスで提供するコーヒー専門店のことです。

　そして、私はアメリカまで飛行機を乗らなくても、日本にいながらシアトルのインディペンデト系カフェ体験をしてもらいたい気持ちでお店をオープンしました。店舗の内装は、いままで日本のコーヒーショップになかったインダストリアルデザイン（工業的なデザイン）にし、アメリカの工場で使われているイスを使い、鉄筋がむき出しの内装は当時としては斬新なものだったと思います。実際、オープンして数日経っているにも関わらず、毎朝、お店の前を犬の散歩をしている方に、鉄筋が出たままの状態を見られ、「ここのお店はいつ工事が終わるの？」と聞かれたことがあるぐらいです。

　シアトルのカフェ同様、トイレに入るのに鍵を持って行かないとドアが開かいころまで細部にわたって忠実に再現しました。多くの日本人のお客様にはめんどうくさがられましたが、特定のお客様には、「ここまでやる！（笑）」と言われ、とても楽しんでいただけることができました。

　これまで日本の個人店カフェというと、ランチに食事を提供している食事系カフェが主流だったのですが、私のお店は、限られたエスプレッソドリンクとドーナツのみ、ご来店いただいたお客様には、「ここのお店はメニューこれしかないの？」と、たびたび聞かれました。日本は、異常なほど多くの自動販売機・コンビニエンスストアがあり、どこでもコーヒーを安価で飲むことができる世界唯一の国です。ということもあり、日本の個人店カフェの多くは、コーヒーの杯数だけで売上を取るのは難しく、コーヒー以外のフードで客単価を上げるか、フルサービスにしてコーヒー自体の単価を上げるのどちらかで売上を取る方法が主流でした。しかし、シアトルのカフェのようにセルフサービスのコーヒーだけで、渋谷という家賃が安くない店舗がどうすれば成り立たせることができるのか？　それが、私の当時の課題でした。

　日本のコーヒー価格は、フルサービスのコーヒーは高く、セルフサービスのコーヒーは安いというルールがまかり通っている業界や世間の当時の常識を疑い、セルフサービスのテイクアウトでも世界一高価なコーヒーを提供する手法を考えました。それはオープンキッチンにして、お客様にラテアートをしている様子を見ていただき、そのご鑑賞料金を付加価値としてコーヒーの価格をフルサービス並みにしました。この発想は、日本のお寿司屋と天ぷら屋からきたものです。カウンターの前で握るお寿司や目の前で天ぷらを揚げるのは、決して安くはありません。逆に高いものです。そしてまた、カウンターでの様子がライブアートに見えたのです！

　これまで、セルフサービスのテイクアウトコーヒーは、店員さんが安全のためカップにフタをつけてお客様に提供していましたが、私はテイクアウト用のペーパーカップでもすべてラテアートのライブアートを行い、提供し、お客様ご自身でフタをしていただきました。日本のコーヒーショップではみな制服を着ていた時代に、私服であるSupremeのビーニーキャップ、Tシャツ、短パンでコーヒーを淹れるという独自のバリスタファッションのスタイルを確立しました。つねにすべて誰もやっていないこと、前例がないことへの挑戦です。

　2011年に起きた東日本大震災が落ち着き出したころから、東京には、インディペンデント系カフェが急増し、いまでは私が日本でやっていたことは主流になっています。現在、東京では、ペーパーカップにラテアートが描かれていることや、襟のないTシャツでコーヒーを淹れている様子は珍しくありません。また、日本のお客様も以前よりずいぶんコーヒーにお金を使うようになりました。

　東京で初めてお店をオープンしてから6年後、2015年12月に、アメリカのシカゴに sawada coffee をオープンしました。日本で唯一のお店から、世界で唯一のお店へのステップアップです。

　この sawada coffee は、いままでの経験を踏まえ、失敗や上手くいったこと、そして、いまの自分自身の考えをもとにオープンしました。これからお店を開店させる方や、現在お店をオープンされている方に、その店舗作りの内容や考え方を知っていただき、少しでも参考になりましたら幸いです。

2016年10月　澤田洋史

14	**Chapter 1** ## CONCEPT コンセプト	74	**Chapter 4** ## THE MACHINE マシーンや器具

14 Chapter 1
CONCEPT
コンセプト

16 A clear goal determines the shop's concept
明確な目標が店のコンセプトになる

19 "the world's most 'delightful' coffee shop"
世界で一番"楽しい"コーヒーショップとは？

26 The concept of sawada coffee
sawada coffeeのコンセプト

28 Be different
他店と差別化する

30 Chapter 2
SHOP DESIGN
ショップデザイン

32 Creating a symbolic shop logo
店の肝となるショップロゴをつくる

34 Exterior
店舗の外装

36 Entrance
エントランス

38 Interior
店舗の内装

40 Key interior decoration
キーとなる内装例

56 Chapter 3
THE MENU
メニュー

58 A winning menu
店の決め手となるメニュー

60 Menu advice
メニュー作りのポイント

62 Signature item
看板メニュー

72 Free pour latte art
フリーポアラテアートについて

74 Chapter 4
THE MACHINE
マシーンや器具

76 Selecting the machine and tools
マシーン・器具の選定

78 The purpose of investing in the machine
マシーンに投資する理由

82 The machine
マシーン紹介

86 The barista gear
器具紹介

90 Chapter 5
OPERATIONS
オペレーション

92 How to pour latte art
ラテアートの出し方

94 A place that stimulates your five senses
五感を刺激するオペレーション

104 Why do I insist on free pour latte art?
なぜ、私は「フリーポアラテアート」にこだわるのか？

106 Positioning the right amount of staff
スタッフを配置する

112 Opening hours
営業時間

114 Chapter 6
LOCATION
ロケーション

116 How to open a coffee shop without avoiding competitors
競合店が集まるエリアに出店する

120 | **Chapter 7**
BRANDING
ブランディング

122 | **Brand philosophy**
ブランドの考え方

124 | **Brand strategy for independent coffee shops**
個人経営のコーヒーショップが必要な6つのブランド戦略

126 | **Offer something new and original**
体験したことがないものを提供する

128 | **Focus on a specific target clientele**
来ていただきたいお客様に集中する

130 | **The sole purpose of a business is to serve the customer**
商売とは、お客様のためにあります

132 | **The branding pyramid**
顧客ブランディングピラミッド

134 | **The staff should be a part of the brand**
スタッフにもブランディングは必要

136 | **Chapter 8**
BARISTA
バリスタ

138 | **The ideal barista**
理想のバリスタ像

140 | **The Barista Championship**
バリスタチャンピオンシップについて

142 | **Barista requirements to demonstrate the skills at the championship**
チャンピオンシップで実力が発揮できるバリスタの条件

sawada coffee style
CONTENTS

Chapter 1
CONCEPT
第1章 コンセプト

店づくりで、第一に考えたいのはコンセプトだ。どんな店にしたいのかという目標や目的を明確にさせることは、店の骨格となり、店名にもつながる重要な要素となる。そして、その後のショップデザインからメニュー、ロケーション、ロゴまで店の作りをスムーズにさせる。著者自身の目標を例にあげて、コンセプトを考えてみよう

Chapter 1 **CONCEPT**

A clear goal determines the shop's concept
明確な目標が店のコンセプトになる

When trying to identify the concept of a coffee shop, the first and foremost thing to do is to question why you want to start a business. The goal must be clear. For example, my personal goal and purpose is creating "the world's most 'delightful' coffee shop".

What does the world's most "delightful" mean
- To offer the most delicious and enjoyable coffee experience.
- To offer unrivaled service and value.
- To provide a clean and very comfortable environment.
- To create a work environment where the staff truly enjoy what they're doing.

Once you have set high goals and purposes, it will become clear what you need to do on a day-to-day basis in order to achieve your goal.
A job simply turns into tedious labour when you don't need to think about it everyday. I believe that fulfilling the mission, whereby the shop contributes to society, is the ultimate raison d'etre. Setting a simple goal easily reached with very little effort is not a high goal. An easily attainable goal with quick results only provides instantaneous satisfaction which hinders growth of both oneself and the business. Being satisfied with the status quo also makes keeping the status quo that much harder.

By identifying your goal, or specifically, what kind of coffee shop you want to create, the concept will present itself.
Once you have a clear concept, details such as the shop design (interior and exterior), menu list, service operations, target customer, location, opening hours and desired staff will fall into place.

コンセプトを考えるには、まず、なんのためにコーヒーショップを始めるのか？
その目標を明確にする必要があります。私が考える目標、目的は、「世界で一番"楽しい"コーヒーショップ」をつくるということです。

世界で一番"楽しい"の意味とは
・世界で一番おいしく楽しいコーヒー体験
・世界で一番楽しく気持ちのいいサービスと価値を提供する
・世界で一番きれいで居心地のよいお店
・世界で一番スタッフ全員が楽しく働けるコーヒーショップ

目標、目的を高く持つと、なにをしなければいけないのか日々考えることができます。
日々考えないでいると、仕事ではなく単なる楽しくない作業になります。使命を実現し、お店は社会に貢献できてこそ、存在意義があります。少し頑張ったら、到達できそうな簡単な目標は、高い目標ではありません。目標がすぐに達成可能なものにしてしまうと、達成した時点で満足してしまい、自身もお店舗も成長はありません。また、現状に満足すると、現状維持も難しくなります。

目的を明確にすると、どのようなお店をつくるか、コンセプトが明確になります。
明確なコンセプトがあると、そのコンセプトにあったショップデザイン（店舗内装・外装）、メニュー、オペレーション（サービス方法）、ターゲット、ロケーション、営業時間、スタッフが決まります。

To offer the most delicious and enjoyable coffee experience

世界で一番おいしく楽しいコーヒー体験

Not only should the coffee be delicious, but it should also be original and fun in appearance.
おいしいコーヒーを提供するだけでなく、斬新で見た目にも楽しいコーヒーを提供する。

Chapter 1 **CONCEPT**

"the world's most 'delightful' coffee shop"
世界で一番"楽しい"コーヒーショップとは?

Great service and warm communication between staff and customers.
気持ちのよいサービスとスタッフとお客様との楽しい会話。

Chapter 1　**CONCEPT**

"the world's most 'delightful' coffee shop"
世界で一番"楽しい"コーヒーショップとは?

To offer unrivaled service and value.

世界で一番楽しく
気持ちのよいサービスと
価値を提供する

"the world's most 'delightful' coffee shop"
世界で一番"楽しい"コーヒーショップとは?

To provide a clean and very comfortable environment.

世界で一番きれいで居心地のよいお店

Offer a mellow, relaxing space to enjoy both coffee and pleasant conversation.
くつろいでコーヒーを飲むことができる場所と、お客様同士が楽しい会話をすることができるお店。

Chapter 1 **CONCEPT**

The concept of sawada coffee
sawada coffee のコンセプト

The concept of "sawada coffee USA" is: "the one and only coffee shop in the world incorporating Japanese culture". It is important to name the business in accordance to the concept. "Sawada coffee" is a coffee shop brand from the US. I decided to name my business using my surname, "Sawada", in the same fashion as world famous Japanese brands such as Honda or Mazda, in the wish to reach my ambitious goal of associating "sawada coffee" to mean the one and only coffee shop in the world incorporating Japanese culture.

---

sawada coffee USA のコンセプトは、「日本のカルチャーを盛り込んだ世界唯一のコーヒーショップ」です。店の名はコンセプトをもとに合うように名づける必要があります。
sawada coffee は、アメリカ発のコーヒーショップブランドです。sawadaつまりサワダ は、私の苗字ですが、世界の誰もが知る日本ブランド HONDA（ホンダ）や、MAZDA（マツダ）があるように、「世界で唯一」を目指し、加えて日本のカルチャーを盛り込んだコーヒーショップを意味する高い目標から名づけました。

sawada coffee style

Chapter 1　**CONCEPT**

Be different
他店と差別化する

Never waver from the concept and strive to be the one and only original coffee shop.

Present day Tokyo has seen an upsurge in the sheer number of coffee shops with similar menus and design. It seems that the only difference is the name and location. People may follow a trend such as "micro-roasters are gaining popularity" or "coffee stands in apparel shops are trending"… However, there is no hope in gaining success from simply adapting to a trend. There is no existential value if the business is just copying someone else's concept or idea. You need to possess the drive and will to transform the industry by creating an innovative idea altering the norm of what a customer expects, while understanding the changes in the world.

Key points to consider
- **Ideas are important**
- **Having an original sales point is a must**
- **Never copy what others do**
- **Never follow what others do**

The above list is what I bear in mind while striving to accomplish my goal. Copying another's idea results in losing your own pride as well as those working with you.

自店のコンセプトから外れず、ほかのコーヒーショップとは違う世界唯一のお店を目指す

現在東京にはメニュー、ショップデザインが同じようなコーヒーショップが乱立しています。違うのは店名と場所だけのような店舗のことです。世の中は、「マイクロロースターに人気が高まっている」とか、「アパレルショップにコーヒースタンドが流行りだ」などといった流行や変化にそのまま対応していては、成功は見込めません。誰かのものまねでは、お店の存在価値がありません。世の中の変化を理解したうえで、自らのアイデアで、お客様の常識や習慣を変えるぐらいのイノベーションを起こし、自らの力で世の中や業界に変化を創るぐらいの行動力が必要です。

そのためには
- **アイデアが重要**
- **他店にない自店のセールスポイントが必要**
- **ほかのコーヒーショップの横並びやモノマネは絶対にしない**
- **ほかのコーヒーショップに追随してはいけない**

ということを念頭に目指していきたいものと考えます。
パクリは自分自身だけでなく、そこで働くスタッフのプライドもなくなります。

Chapter 2
SHOP DESIGN

第2章　ショップデザイン

第1章で述べたように店の目標が決まったら、おのずと店名も決まってきたはずだ。ここでは、コンセプトに基づく店のデザインはどのようにすべきかを説明する。店の顔となるロゴから外装、内装ではテーブル席からスタッフが動きやすい動線づくりまで、ショップデザインについてノウハウを紹介。

vada
offee
USA

Chapter 2　SHOP DESIGN

Creating a symbolic shop logo
店の肝となるショップロゴをつくる

Once you have named the shop, the next step is creating the logo based on the name. It is crucial to pay particular attention to minute details of the logo design. Often times, perhaps in order to save costs, people create a logo themselves with built in fonts from their computer, or ask a friend who has very little experience in design. Although it is understandable, it is imperative to hire a seasoned professional designer who understands the concept, to help create not only the logo but also the signage, shop cards, stickers, business cards, website design, etc. Never underestimate how customers notice the smallest of details. They possess a sharp eye and their perception makes or breaks their impression of the shop's taste and concept. An attractive shop has been designed with meticulous calculation. In doing so, customers are more inclined to take home original giveaways to give to friends or, for example, to use stickers on personal items, thereby creating free advertisement.

Use money wisely by avoiding wasteful expenses and instead spend as much as necessary on the things that really matter.

ショップ名が決まったら、それをもとにショップロゴをつくります。ショップロゴのデザインでは、ディテールのこだわりはとても重要です。よく見られるのは、お金をかけたくない理由からか、「家のパソコンの書体でロゴを作った」とか、「デザインを少しかじっている程度の友達に依頼した」というパターンです。やはり、ここはコストをかけてもプロのデザイナーにロゴを含むデザインすべて（看板、ショップカード、ステッカー、名刺、ホームページなど）を、店のコンセプトを伝えて、その道のプロに依頼しなくてはいけません。お客様は、細かなディテールをよく見ています。そこからお店のポリシーやセンスを感じとっているのです。魅力的な店舗は、ショップデザインのすべてが計算されています。そんな理由でお客様は、ショップカードやステッカーなどを持ち帰り、友人などに配ってくれたり、ステッカーを自分の私物に貼ったりして店舗の宣伝をしてくれるのです。

お金は必要なところにしっかりかけて、無駄なところにはお金はかけない。

sawada coffee logo   A

sawada coffee

sawada
coffee

sawada coffee
CHICAGO, USA

sawada
coffee
CHICAGO, USA

sawada coffee
USA

sawada
coffee
USA

Chapter 2 **SHOP DESIGN**

Exterior
店舗の外装

A bold mural painted by a local artist. The interior of the shop is hidden by the wall to avoid onlookers from the street.

地元アーティストが描いたインパクトある外壁。通行人の目線は、壁で店内の様子を見ることができない。

Chapter 2 **SHOP DESIGN**

Entrance
エントランス

In defiance of the traditional coffee shop entrance.
いままでのコーヒーショップの常識を覆すエントランス

The entrance is a sturdy, simple steel door which I intentionally made difficult to find with no visible signage. In making the entrance rather unapproachable at first look to a passerby, I wanted to recreate a sense of a special, private hideaway only for those "in the know".

落書きそのままに鉄の扉のみのエントランス。立て看板もなく、入口がどこにあるのか、わざとわかりにくくする。一般の通行人には入りづらく、知った人間しか入れない。一見、「こちらは会員制のクラブです。限られたお客様のみ」を思わせる入口。

Entering through the steel door, a strange staircase appears and only those undaunted will proceed. The atmosphere is somewhat similar to a secret watering hole during the days of prohibition, peaking the interest of the curious. Some may even wonder, is this an illegal outfit?

エントランスを進むと、さらに怪しげな階段があり、感度の高いお客様の客層のみに絞り込む。禁酒法時代の隠れた酒場のような秘密の入口。通のお客様のツボを刺激する。「なかでは、麻薬の密造をしているのか？」。

Interior
店舗の内装

The shop is a converted old warehouse and by retaining much of the original structure and atmosphere, I managed to minimize renovation costs.

もとは古い倉庫だった店内。そのままのよい雰囲気を残し、投資を最小限に抑えた。

sawada coffee style

Chapter 2 **SHOP DESIGN**

Key interior decoration
キーとなる内装例

Ping-pong table seats
卓球台のテーブル席

A community "ping pong table" seat where customers and baristas can actually enjoy a good match together.

お客様同士、バリスタとお客様の卓球対戦もできるコミュニティテーブル席。

Chapter 2 **SHOP DESIGN**

Key interior decoration
キーとなる内装例

Counter seats
カウンター席

Counter seats placed along the window allows customers to enjoy a view of the street from above.

窓から外を見下ろせるカウンター席。

Chapter 2 **SHOP DESIGN**

Key interior decoration
キーとなる内装例

Pinball machine
ピンボールマシーン

A coffee shop is not only a peaceful haven for adults. The pinball machine is placed for both adults and children to enjoy.

コーヒーショップは大人だけの憩いの場ではない。大人も子どもも楽しめるピンボールマシーンを配置。

Condiment bar
コンディメントバー

Condiments such as sugar and milk are placed on the counter. An original Hiroshi Sawada signature model skateboard manufactured by Chicago's local "Blue Town Skateboard" hangs on the wall.

砂糖やミルクなどを置いたカウンター。地元シカゴのスケートボードブランド「Blue Town Skateboard」のHiroshi Sawadaモデルを壁に設置。

Chapter 2 **SHOP DESIGN**

Key interior decoration
キーとなる内装例

Drip station
ドリップステーション

A custom-made skateboard drip station produced by HARIO x Hiroshi Sawada. The stand is removable and baristas can use the skateboard to commute,

HARIO x Hiroshi Sawadaのカスタムスケートボード・ドリップステーション。スタンドの取り外しが可能で、実際にバリスタがこのスケートボードで通勤も可能。

Chapter 2 **SHOP DESIGN**

Key interior decoration

キーとなる内装例

Food display
フードディスプレー

Popular local doughnuts, such as the camo patterned "military doughnut", are tastefully displayed.

迷彩柄にデザインされたミリタリードーナツなど、地元でもおいしいと評判のドーナッツをおいしそうに飾る。

Chapter 2 **SHOP DESIGN**

Key interior decoration
キーとなる内装例

Punching bag
Supreme / Everlast Leather Heavy Bag
サンドバッグ

A punching bag hangs from the shop's ceiling.
Customers can relieve stress by punching the bag while enjoying coffee.

天井から、ボクシング用サンドバッグが釣りさがる店内。
コーヒーを飲みながらパンチしてストレス発散できる。

SAWADA's coffee shop style

Chapter 2 **SHOP DESIGN**

Key interior decoration

キーとなる内装例

Behind the counter
カウンター内

Equipment and food is placed to ensure seamless movement.

バリスタが動きやすいよう機器や食材を配置。

Chapter 2 **SHOP DESIGN**

Key interior decoration
キーとなる内装例

Backyard
バックヤード

Food is stored in a clean and orderly fashion for easy access and upkeep of stock.

食材は出し入れしやすく、オーダー数（必要数量）をわかりやすく、清潔に整頓する。

Restrooms
トイレ

intervals to maintain a clean and sanitary environment.

つねに清潔で衛生管理できるよう、決まった時間に確認する。

Chapter 3
THE MENU

第3章　メニュー

3^{25}

3^{50}　　　　　　4^{00}

2^{50}

2^{00}　　　　　　2^{50}

4^{50}

MERS・$1 SHOTS・

お客様が他店に流れないためにメニュー作りにはポイントがある。高い基準の商品を提供はもちろん。価格で競争しない、エスプレッソマシーンでつくる商品をメインにする、メニューを豊富にしないこともあげられる。その理由は廃棄ロスを出さない以外の理由として店の売りがはっきりとお客様に伝わるからである。

Chapter 3　**THE MENU**

A winning menu
店の決め手となるメニュー

Take the customer perspective in creating a world class high quality menu – don't settle with an "okay" menu from personal standards.

Any eatery or drinking establishment servicing high standard products from the customer's point of view, has a distinct advantage compared to the others in the industry. As world class standards become common and customers more knowledgeable, they will naturally begin to avoid lesser quality products and ultimately lose interest in going to shops serving such sub-standard products. However, it is difficult to discern or distinguish standards when it comes to coffee as there is a multitude of variety of coffee beans, roasting methods, and of course, personal taste. At sawada coffee, we strive to serve irresistible items, easily recognizable and customized to the local palate.

**メニューは「自分の基準」ではなく、
「お客様から見て高い基準。世界基準」を目指す**

飲食店すべてお客様から見て「本当に高い基準」で商品を提供することができるとほかの店舗を圧倒する商品力になります。世界に通用する本物の高い基準がお客様の常識になり、お客様はその基準に達していない商品には手を出さなくなり、他店に行く気がなくなります。コーヒーそのものは、豆の種類や焙煎度合等で味に好みがあるため明確なおいしさの基準を持たせることは難しく、おいしさの定義は人それぞれです。sawada coffeeでは、アメリカに適応した、お客様に伝わりやすい、圧倒的な商品力をつくることを重視しています。

Chapter 3　**THE MENU**

Menu advice
メニュー作りのポイント

Compete with the major chain-stores with originality

Customers who favor low cost over quality taste and service do not match my store concept. In other words, I am not conducting a business competing with low prices. Only large scale coffee chain stores and convenience stores are able to compete with prices by lowering their costs with bulk purchases. Therefore, in order to successfully run an independent café, originality is the key.

The feature items on the menu should be something prepared with the espresso machine

Espresso machines and espresso grinders nowadays are very high performance, enabling the barista to prepare individual orders without a long waiting time. It also means that there is minimum loss because each item is prepared after an order is placed. In other words, there are no pre-prepared items on the menu.

Narrowing down the menu

No successful café with main featuring items has a long menu. It may seem that the more variety and number of items there are on a menu, the more there is to satisfy and please the customer, but instead, it results in loss of focus and mediocre service. It is similar to that of any highly popular ramen shop, where they too offer only a limited menu. In addition, the more items there are on a menu, the more space and workload is required resulting in a loss of both time and product waste. It is much more gratifying if the barista trains and perfects the skills for a limited number of items, therefore providing a higher quality output, which in turn results in higher customer satisfaction. For example, major Japanese electrical appliance manufacturers sell numerous mediocre products, whereas, Apple or Dyson focus on a very limited number of dominant products. Needless to say, that the latter is in the lead in terms of sales revenue.

Chapter 3　**THE MENU**

Increase of menu items
メニューを増やす

Increase of labor and loss
手間とロスが増える

A vicious cycle depicted of a menu with too many items
多すぎるメニューでの悪いサークル

Decrease in service and product quality
商品力とサービスが落ちる

Lose focus on the sales point
なにが売りかわからなくなる

Decrease in revenue
売上が下がる

大手チェーン店ができない質で勝負する

味やサービスはそこそこで、価格が安いほうに流れるお客様は私のお店のコンセプトに合わないともいえます。つまり低価格で勝負するところでは商売を見ていないのです。価格で競争できるのは、スケールメリットを活かして仕入れコストを下げることができる多店舗展開している大手コーヒーチェーン店やコンビニエンスストアぐらいでしょう。勝負は自分自身の店の持ち味が決めてとなります。

エスプレッソマシーンでつくるメニューがメイン商品

現在、エスプレッソマシーンやエスプレッソグラインダーは高性能でお客様からオーダーがあってからつくりだしても長く待たせることはありません。また、オーダーを受けてからつくりだすので、商品ロスが出ないのも特徴です。要するにつくりおきメニューがないのです。

商品数を絞り込む

強力な商品を提供している店舗では、メニューが豊富な店はありません。メニュー数が多いことで多くのお客様に喜んでもらえると考えがちですが、結局のところは、すべての商品が中途半端になり、なにが売りなのかわからなくなります。アップル社やダイソン社は、少ない商品数で、圧倒的な商品力を打ち出し、日本の大手家電メーカーは、鳴かず飛ばずの多くの商品数を発売しているように現在の業績を見ればわかるはずです。

Chapter 3　**THE MENU**

Signature item
看板メニュー

A signature item on the menu should be original and unique, even attracting non-local customers.

- Pique the interest with the naming.
- Visually impressive, making the customer want to photograph, share and post on their SNS pages such as Instagram.

看板商品は、おいしさ、珍しさ目当てで遠方からでも来店したくなるメニューのことをいいます。

・「これはなんだろう？」と思わせるメニュー名で興味を持たせる。
・お客様が撮影したくなる見た目のインパクトがあるとInstagramなど、SNSで拡散されます。

sawada coffee's signature menu

Military Latte

The Military Latte is a visually impressive drink designed in a camouflage pattern, combining premium Japanese Matcha and homemade vanilla syrup with perfectly dripped espresso.

看板メニュー
ミリタリーラテ

最高級の抹茶と、自家製バニラシロップ、エスプレッソを合わせ、迷彩柄に仕上げた見た目にもインパクトあるドリンク。

sawada coffee's signature menu

Tokyo Style Cold Brew

Served in a Japanese traditional "Masu" style cup, the slow brewed iced coffee is combined with Japanese brown sugar syrup.
(Also available in bottles for take-outs)

看板メニュー
コールドブリュー・東京スタイル
長時間かけてていねいに水出ししたアイスコーヒーに黒蜜を合わせ、日本の桝酒のように提供(テイクアウト用のボトル入りも販売)。

sawada coffee's signature menu

Steamed Sake

Steamed Sake is hot sake, heated by the espresso machine's steam wand. This is a menu item which utilizes a main feature of the espresso machine.

看板メニュー
スチームドサケ
エスプレッソマシーンのスチームワンドで温めた熱燗。
エスプレッソマシーンを最大限に利用したメニュー。

sawada coffee's signature menu

Military Donuts

An original, order-made doughnut from Chicago's highly popular "DOUGHNUT VAULT", it is designed in a camouflage pattern with a mixture of Japanese Matcha, salted caramel and chocolate.

看板メニュー

ミリタリードーナツ

シカゴでは行列が絶えないドーナツショップ「DOUGHNUT・VAULT」に別注した、抹茶、塩キャラメル、チョコレートで迷彩柄にしたドーナツ。

Chapter 3 THE MENU

Free pour latte art
フリーポアラテアートについて

As it is said that "The beauty of free pour latte art is proof of its deliciousness", we thrive to provide world class latte art, overwhelming the competition.

- For high quality art, a vivid and clear espresso background and smooth textured crema is important = the barista must possess the skills to prepare the perfect espresso.
- The foam milk must be silky and smooth = the barista must possess advanced steaming techniques.

Beautiful artwork is prepared with the combination of espresso and foam milk, resulting in a tasty, rich and silky smooth café latte which melts in your mouth.

Compatibility

When offering café latte as part of the menu, in addition to paying attention to the quality of the coffee beans and milk, it is equally important to use coffee beans that complement and balance well with milk.

It is best to offer a food menu that enhances the taste of the signature or promoted item. For instance, if the cafe wants to focus on a milk based drink such as a latte, it is prudent to offer chocolate or cinnamon flavored items that perfectly match with the drink. Similar to the concept that milk does not go well with Japanese school lunches, a food menu need not consist of sandwiches and hotdogs, etc.

"フリーポアラテアートの美しさはおいしさの証明"通り、世界基準のラテアートで他店を圧倒する

・アートの背景となるエスプレッソの抽出カラーが鮮明でクレマのキメが細かい。つまり、バリスタの高度な抽出技術が必要。
・フォームミルクの泡のキメが細かく光沢がある。つまり、バリスタの高度なスチーミングテクニックが必要。

よって、上記のエスプレッソとフォームミルクで、美しいアートが描かれ、コーヒーの風味が非常に豊かで舌にまとわりつくほどのシルキーな泡のカフェラテが完成します。

フードメニューとの相性を考える

カフェラテを提供する場合、コーヒー豆とミルクの品質にこだわることはもちろんですが、ミルクとの相性、バランスを考えたコーヒー豆を用意しなければいけません。

看板商品、売りたい商品をさらにおいしくする相性のよいフードメニューを用意します。たとえば、カフェラテなどミルクを使ったドリンクメニューを売りたい場合は、ミルクとの相性のよいチョコレート系やシナモン風味のスイーツなどにフードメニューに絞り込んでいくのですが、日本の学校給食に牛乳が合わないのと同じでタマゴサンドや、ホットドックなどの食事メニューではないのです。

Chapter 4
THE MACHINE

第 4 章　マシーンや器具

一番コストを落としていけないのは、調理器具である。とくに店の看板メニューを作るエスプレッソマシーンやエスプレッソグラインダーには性能を重視すべきである。同時にそれらを使いこなすバリスタの技量も問われていくわけだが、ここでは、機器についての選ぶ上で重要なポイントと機器の紹介をする。

2·⁰⁰   2·⁵⁰   3·⁰⁰   4·⁰⁰ $1

4·⁵⁰

• $1 SHOTS • $2-$4 TEA •

Chapter 4　**THE MACHINE**

Selecting the machine and tools
マシーン・器具の選定

The selection of equipment and tools is the key to success.

First class chefs select high quality cooking devices as does a barista with equipment and tools. Chefs maintain their knives in top condition by regular sharpening in the same way baristas care for their devices and equipment. The quality of coffee depends highly on the selection of equipment and tools as well as maintenance. One should invest in the best available high performance espresso machine on the market. The performance of an espresso machine is congruent to the price but never settle for less than the best in order to save costs.
Please note, however, that a fully automated coffee machine often used at major coffee chain stores are expensive but do not produce high quality coffee.

マシーン、器具選びが重要な理由

一流の料理人が一流の調理器具を選び、一流のバリスタは一流のマシーン・器具を使います。料理人は包丁を研ぎ、切れ味を保ち、バリスタもていねいに手入れをしながらマシーン・器具を大切に使います。なぜなら、マシーン・器具の選定、メンテナンスの仕方で、提供するドリンクの質がまったく変わるからです。エスプレッソマシーンは高性能な最高レベルのマシーンを選びます。エスプレッソマシーンの性能は価格と比例しますが、投資をケチってはいけません。
※ただし、チェーン店が使用するボタンひとつでコーヒーが淹れられるフルオートマチックマシーンは高価ですが、味は比例していません。

Chapter 4　**THE MACHINE**

The purpose of investing in the machine
マシーンに投資する理由

The performance of the equipment is essential to the taste of the coffee

The taste of coffee is a result of three elements; the performance of the machine, the technical skills of the barista, and the quality of the coffee beans. For instance, even if you use the most rare and expensive coffee beans, you cannot bring out the best if you are using a low quality espresso grinder. Moreover, even if you have an expensive, high performing espresso machine, without the technical skills of the barista, you cannot maximize the benefits of using that machine. It is similar to a novice driver driving a Formula 1 racing car.

コーヒーの味には、マシーンの性能が不可欠

コーヒーの味は、「マシーンの性能」「バリスタの技量」「コーヒー豆の質」の3つレベルで決まります。たとえば、いくら高価で希少なコーヒー豆を使ってもエスプレッソグラインダーの性能が低いと、そのコーヒー豆の味を最大限に抽出することはできません。また、いくら高価で高性能なエスプレッソマシーンでもバリスタの技量が低いとマシーンを最大限に使いこなすことはできません。F1レーシングマシーンに、自動車運転初心者が乗るのと同じです。バリスタの技量が高くても、性能が低いエスプレッソマシーンだと思うような素晴らしいエスプレッソやミルクフォームは期待できません。F1レーサーが軽自動車でレースに出場するようなものです。

Chapter 4　THE MACHINE

The purpose of investing in the machine
マシーンに投資する理由

High level machines bring high level barista applications.

In order to hire highly skilled or motivated baristas, you should purchase a quality machine equivalent to that used at barista world championships. A barista who is knowledgeable and recognizes quality machines will apply for position openings at such cafes.

High level machines bring customers

Coffee connoisseurs also visit cafes using quality espresso machines and grinders because they are able to imagine the taste simply from the machine's manufacturer and model. Customers do not want to drink coffee of the same level they can prepare at home. The customer is looking to experience a taste which cannot be made at home or bought from a vending machine, convenience store or main-stream coffee shop.

ハイレベルのマシーンを見てバリスタは応募してくる

最初から技量の高いバリスタや、向上心が高いバリスタを採用したい場合は、バリスタの世界大会で使用されているレベルのマシーンを購入しなければいけません。また、それをわかっているバリスタは、お店に設置されているマシーンを見て店舗の採用募集に応募してきます。

お客様もマシーンのレベルで来店する

通のお客様も、エスプレッソマシーンやグラインダーを見て来店します。わかっているお客様はマシーンのメーカーやモデルで味が想像できるのです。お客様は、家庭用エスプレッソマシーンのレベルのコーヒーをわざわざお店に来て飲みたくありません。お客様は自宅、自動販売機、大手コーヒーチェーン店、コンビニエンスストアで体験できない味を求めているのです。

Chapter 4　THE MACHINE

The machine
マシーン紹介

A custom graphic design painted directly by a local graphic artist from Chicago.
地元シカゴのアーティストによるグラフィックを直接ペインティングされた特別カスタムモデル。

Espresso Machine

VICTORIA ARDUINO Black Eagle
VICTORIA ARDUINO is the official espresso machine used at the WBC (World Barista Championship). Ambitious baristas dreaming to one day become a world champion wish to use a high performance machine enabling them to train while they work.

エスプレッソマシーン

VICTORIA ARDUINO　Black Eagle
WBC（ワールド・バリスタ・チャンピオンシップ）のオフィシャルエスプレッソマシーン。チャンピンシップを目指すような向上心の高いバリスタは、チャンピオンシップ公式の高性能マシーンを望んでいます。毎日の営業時間がトレーニングになるからです。

Chapter 4 **THE MACHINE**

The machine
マシーン紹介

Espresso Grinder

Nuova SIMONELLI MYTHOS
Nuova SIMONELLI MYTHOS is a high quality espresso grinder equipped with a cooling fan and heater to enable grinding coffee beans at a uniform temperature. It is also equipped with an anti-static feature preventing the ground powder to clump and additionally prevents the loss of coffee beans caused by any grinding irregularities.

エスプレッソグラインダー

Nuova SIMONELLI MYTHOS
クーリングファンとヒーターを内蔵し、コーヒー豆の挽く温度を均一にする機能や、粉がダマにならない静電気防止機能を兼ね備えた高性能エスプレッソグラインダー。挽き量のブレもないので、コーヒー豆のロスもない。

Chapter 4　THE MACHINE

The barista gear
器具紹介

Tamper

Espresso Parts x Hiroshi Sawada Tamper
Because a tamper is considered a barista's fashion item, the design as well as the performance is important.

タンパー

エスプレッソパーツ×ヒロシサワダ　タンパー
タンパーは、機能性だけでなくデザイン性も重要。バリスタのファッションアイテムのひとつでもある。

Milk Pitcher

HARIO x Hiroshi Sawada Free Pour Latte Art Pitcher
The world's first ultra-lightweight milk pitcher made of reinforced plastic. Unlike a stainless steel pitcher, it does not reach high temperatures, therefore milk does not adhere to the inside which allows smoother pouring. The spout of the pitcher is an original, designed for delicate latte art.

ミルクピッチャー

ハリオ×ヒロシサワダ フリーポアラテアート ピッチャー
世界初の強化プラスチック製の超軽量ミルクピッチャー。ステンレス製ピッチャーのように高温にならないので、内側にミルクのこびりつきがなく注ぎがスムーズ。注ぎ口は繊細なラテアートが描くことができるよう独自の設計になっている。

The barista gear
器具紹介

Skateboard hand drip

HARIO x Hiroshi Sawada Skateboard Pour Over Stand
The legs of the stand can be stored in the removable skateboard and the skateboard can be detached and used.

スケートボードハンドドリップ

ハリオ x ヒロシサワダ スケートボード ポアオーバースタンド
スタンドの脚は、取り外しスケートボード内に収納でき、実際に乗ることも可能。

Kettle

HARIO x Hiroshi Sawada V60 Buono Kettle
A custom model kettle specially painted matte black attached with a VANS BMX grip.

ケトル

ハリオ x ヒロシサワダ V60 ドリップケトル ヴォーノ
マットブラックに特別塗装されたケトル。グリップはVANSのBMXグリップを装着した特別カスタムモデル。

Chapter 5
OPERATIONS

第5章　オペレーション

オペレーションとは、スタッフ通して、またサービスする飲み物に至るまで、すべてに渡って、気持ちよく飲んでいただくためのお客様への対応をいいます。五感を刺激するための舞台作りからラテアートの出し方、適正スタッフの考え方、舞台を盛り上げるレジ担当とバリスタの役割、営業時間までを紹介する。

How to pour latte art
ラテアートの出し方

✗

Holding with the wrong hand
持ち手が逆

Always place the handle of the cup on the right hand side of you and shop logo facing forwards so that when customers share their photos via SNS, it is recognizable. Remember that customers are a viable marketing tool.

つねにラテアートの正面にカップの取手が右、ショップロゴが前面にあること。お客様が撮影し、SNSで投稿する際に認識されます。お客様はお店の営業マンです。

Correct form (Right way to stand)
正しい正面

Chapter 5 OPERATIONS

A place that stimulates your five senses

五感を刺激するオペレーション

An open kitchen and self-service operation to stimulate the five senses.

お客様の五感を、オープンキッチンとセルフサービスにより刺激する。

Look 見る

Presenting the process of preparing a drink in front of the customer exposes the barista's technique and beauty of latte art. The counter of an espresso bar is a barista's stage and the barista must focus on how to entertain the audience. A simple movement can make the drink appear delicious or distasteful.

バリスタはドリンクをつくっているところを見せる。つまり、技（テクニック）・芸術（ラテアート）・作品（ドリンク）をお客様に披露すること。エスプレッソバーのカウンター内はバリスタの舞台。バリスタはお客様を最大限に楽しませることに集中する。バリスタの動きひとつで、おいしそうに見えたり、まずそうにも見えたりします。

Chapter 5 **OPERATIONS**

A place that stimulates your five senses
五感を刺激するオペレーション

Hear 聞く

Experience the sound of the machines grinding the coffee beans and steaming the milk.

コーヒー豆をグラインダーで挽くサウンド。
ミルクをスチームするサウンドを流す。

Chapter 5 **OPERATIONS**

A place that stimulates your five senses
五感を刺激するオペレーション

Smell 嗅ぐ

Release and surround the shop with the delightful aroma of fresh ground beans and the aroma of fresh poured coffee.

挽きたてのコーヒー豆の香り。コーヒーを抽出しているときの香り。店内をコーヒーの香りで充満させる。

Chapter 5 **OPERATIONS**

A place that stimulates your five senses

五感を刺激するオペレーション

Feel 触れる

Let the customer experience the ultimate silky smooth froth of warm milk on their lips.

究極にキメが細かい滑らかなフォームミルクをお客様の唇に触れていただく。

sawada coffee style

Chapter 5 **OPERATIONS**

A place that stimulates your five senses
五感を刺激するオペレーション

Taste 味わう

Provide the customer the best tasting coffee experience.
最高の一杯をお客様に味わっていただく。

Why do I insist on free pour latte art?

なぜ、私は「フリーポアラテアート」にこだわるのか？

A free pour latte art world champion is not only a barista who creates the most beautiful art. A free pour latte art world champion is also a barista who is able to create the most delicious café latte.

フリーポアラテアートの世界チャンピオンは、「世界で一番美しい芸術性あるアート」を描くだけのバリスタではありません。フリーポアラテアートの世界チャンピオンは、「世界で一番おいしいカフェラテ」を淹れることができるバリスタでもあるのです。

Chapter 5 **OPERATIONS**

The 3 factors in creating beautiful latte art

Coffee beans: Freshly ground
Espresso: Freshly dripped
Foam Milk: Freshly steamed

All need to be fresh. Especially foam milk, which immediately begins to lose texture as soon as the steamer stops. Every second counts as one draws, simply by pouring, with the most delicate of paints before losing its smooth texture.

Freshly poured cafe latte tastes the best!
Freshly poured beer tastes the best!
Freshly prepared Sushi tastes the best!

It is very important to serve the customer in a timely manner to ensure that the latte is topped with silky smooth foamed milk at the right temperature. Just as there is a right temperature for any food or drink, latte should be served at the right temperature considering the customer's preference, season, outside temperature and humidity. From a personal perspective, I feel that it is meaningless to disregard the taste of the latte by taking time creating art with a pick or spoon after pouring the milk. A true artist should pursue and perfect both the beauty and the taste.

Free pour latte art varies on how the milk is poured, the type and date the coffee beans were roasted and many other factors. No art is ever exactly the same so the customer can enjoy and savor each encounter. Simultaneously, the barista is able to see and feel improvement in the art therefore never tire from monotony.

美しい芸術性あるラテアートを描くためには、3つの材料が必要です。

「コーヒー豆：挽きたて」
「エスプレッソ：抽出したて」
「フォームミルク：温めたて」

すべて新鮮で作りたて・淹れたてです。フォームミルクは、スチーミングのミルクの回転を止めた瞬間から滑らかさを失いだします。滑らかなうちに、柔らかい絵の具で、注ぎのみのアートを完成させるのです。

カフェラテは注ぎたてが一番おいしい ＝ 生ビールは注ぎたてが一番おいしい ＝ お寿司は握りたてが一番おいしい

1秒でも早くシルキーなフォームミルクを最適な温度で飲んでいただけるようお客様にお出しするのが必須となります。飲み物や料理には、それぞれおいしい最適な温度があるように、お客様の好み、季節、気温、湿度に合わせた最適な温度で提供しなければいけません。私にとってミルクを注いだ後に、ピックやスプーンなどを使って描くアートは提供時間が遅く、おいしさを無視しているのであり得ないことなのです。本物は見た目だけではなく、中身の味も同時に追求することが必要です。

フリーポアラテアートは、ミルクの注ぎ方、コーヒー豆の焙煎日や種類などで、色彩や柄が異なり、まったくその表情が変わります。ひとつとして同じアートは存在しないので、お客様はそのアートの一期一会を楽しむことができるのです。同時にバリスタは、自身のアートの上達具合を確認ができ、単純作業になりません。

Chapter 5 **OPERATIONS**

Positioning the right amount of staff
スタッフを配置する

Overspending on staffing can weigh heavily on a business. However, spending too little will result in an increase in staff load, diminish the quality of service and maintenance of hygiene and the shop will suffer and ultimately, customers will bear the burden.

無駄な人件費をかけると、経営が圧迫されます。しかし、人件費が低過ぎると、スタッフに負荷が多くなり、サービスの低下や、クリンネスがおろそかになり店舗が荒れていきます。結果、お客様に迷惑をかけてしまいます。

Chapter 5　**OPERATIONS**

Positioning the right amount of staff
スタッフを配置する

Cashier
レジ担当

Cashier requirements

- Must be able to memorize loyal customer names and order preferences as well as be knowledgeable about the menu items.
- Must be able to recommend drinks and sweets according to customer preference.
- Must be able to take an order accurately and relay the order accurately to the barista.
- Must be able to control the speed of taking in orders according to the barista's skills and number of orders.
It is the cashier's responsibility to control the flow and timing of orders so that the barista is able to serve the customers in a timely fashion.

In general, customers are willing to wait in line before an order but are inclined to be more impatient once the order has gone through.

レジを担当者の必要なスキルは、

・常連客の名前、ドリンクの好みはすでに暗記し、商品知識がある
・お客様の好みに合わせたドリンク。ドリンクに合わせたスイーツをオススメできる
・お客様のオーダーを正確に受け、バリスタにオーダーを正確に伝える
・バリスタの技量、オーダー数に合わせて注文を受ける速度をコントロールする
※その際、決してバリスタが所定の時間内に提供できない数のオーダーを次々に受けない。

お客様は、オーダーする前（お金を払う前）は、並んで待ってくれます。ですが、オーダー後（お金を払った後）、注文をした物が遅いと気分が悪くなります。

sawada coffee style　**109**

Chapter 5　OPERATIONS

Positioning the right amount of staff
スタッフを配置する

Barista
バリスタ

Barista requirements

- Must be able to create an order quickly and accurately.
- Must stay calm at all times and consistently serve high quality drinks regardless of the order numbers.
- Must have the ability to engage in pleasant communication with the customer while preparing the order.
- Must possess impressive technical skills to awe the customers.
- Must possess entertainment skills so that customers are able to enjoy their time waiting.
- Must be able to provide an enjoyable "real time show".

Always aim to provide products and service above and beyond the price.

バリスタに必要なスキルは、

・オーダーを早く、正確につくる
・オーダー数が多くても焦らないで、質にこだわり、質にブレがない強いメンタルをもつ
・ドリンクをつくりながら、待っているお客様と楽しいトークでコミュニケーションをとる
・華麗な手さばきをお客様に披露する
・待ち時間も楽しんでいただく、エンターテインメント性がある
・お客様にできたてのシズル感を楽しんでいただく

つねに価格以上の価値ある商品、サービス提供を目指すのが決め手となります。

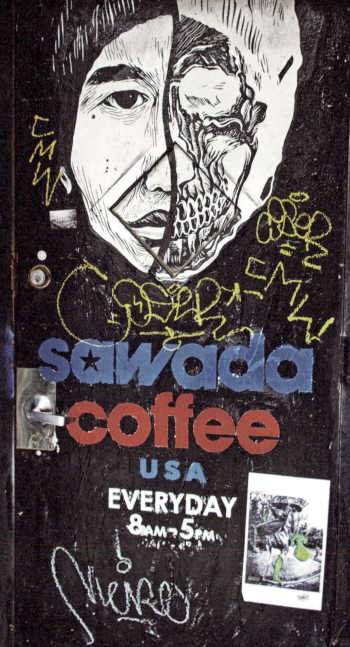

Chapter 5 **OPERATIONS**

Opening hours
営業時間

sawada coffee opening hours		**Sawada coffee 営業時間**
Monday thru Friday	7:00 am - 4:00 pm	月曜日〜金曜日 7:00〜16:00
Saturday and Sunday	8:00 am - 4:00 pm	土曜日・日曜日　8:00〜16:00
*summer time: Everyday	8:00 am - 5:00 pm	（サマータイム　月曜日〜日曜日 8:00〜17:00）

My idea of a healthy coffee shop is one that opens early in the morning and closes early in the evening allowing a balanced and healthy lifestyle for the barista. The shop should be well prepared and open before the morning rush-hour which also means that the barista will perform better throughout the day by commuting in a more relaxed environment. Likewise, by closing in the early evening, the barista is able to avoid the evening rush. Personally, I do not take any caffeine after 5:00pm so that I am able to sleep better.

After 5:00pm, I enjoy having drinks during happy hour. It also allows me to enjoy time to shop since most department stores and boutiques are still open. By going to various restaurants and visiting new places, I feel invigorated, inspired and new ideas are formed as well as good conversation starters with customers. This is the privileged and enjoyable life of being a barista.

Coffee shops required to open for long hours in order to reach target sales revenue is most likely to be located in a high rent area with heavy foot traffic yet lacks attraction. An attractive coffee shop brings in attractive customers who will visit during opening hours.

私の考える健全なコーヒーショップは、早朝にオープンして夕方早く閉店し、バリスタも早寝早起きで健康的あることです。お店は出勤ラッシュ前にオープンしたいものです。ラッシュ前の電車が空いている時間に座って出勤していると、長時間の立ち仕事であるバリスタはよいパフォーマンスを出すことができます。また、帰宅ラッシュの電車にも乗りません。私はよい睡眠に取るため、17:00 以降は、カフェインを取りません。

17:00 以降は、ハッピーアワーを利用して、明るい時間からアルコールを飲みます。デパートやブティックなどもオープンしているのでゆっくりショッピングを楽しむことができます。いろいろなレストランに食事に行ったり、行ったことがない場所に行くと視野も広がり、脳を刺激し、よいアイデアが生まれたり、お客様との会話のネタもつくることができます。これはバリスタの特権で、毎日が楽しく充実した生活になります。

営業時間を長くしないと期待する売上が取れないコーヒーショップは、交通量や通行量が多いだけで集客性を狙った家賃が高いお店か、魅力に欠けるお店だと思います。魅力のあるコーヒーショップには、魅力あるお客様が営業時間内に必ず来店します。

Chapter 6
LOCATION

第6章　ロケーション

どこに店を開くか、これは一番悩ましい問題。自分の店を繁盛店にするには、競合店がいない地域がよいのではないかと考えがちだが、意外にも答えはノーだ。その理由とはなにか、また、どんな地域で店をかまえていくのがベストかについてガイドをする。

Chapter 6 **LOCATION**

How to open a coffee shop without avoiding competitors

競合店が集まるエリアに出店する

Location is the most important factor when opening a coffee shop.

Many people ask me why I opened a coffee shop in Chicago. The answer is because Chicago is one of the top three metropolitan cities in the US and is not only known as the birthplace of "Intelligentsia Coffee" which produced the first World Barista Champion from the US, but many other high quality coffee shops. Therefore, Chicago has many gourmet customers who understand and appreciate good coffee.

By narrowing it down further, there are famous large chain stores like STARBUCKS and La COLOMBE within walking distance. Again, there is also a high concentration of unique restaurants where the locals frequent. It was my aim to open a coffee shop surrounded by competitors.

お店をオープンするのにロケーション選びは重要

「澤田さんは、なぜ米国シカゴにコーヒーショップをオープンしたのですか?」とよく聞かれます。その理由は、シカゴはアメリカ三大都市のひとつで、アメリカ人初のワールドバリスタチャンピオンも輩出した有名店　Intelligentsia Coffee（インテリジェンシア・コーヒー）の1号店を始め、上質なコーヒーショップが多数存在しています。よって、シカゴはコーヒーに対してもグルメなお客様が大勢いるからです。

さらにエリアを限定すると、徒歩圏内にSTARBUCKS（スターバックス）はもちろん、La COLOMBE（ラ・コロンブ）といった競合となる有名店があります。また地元の人が通う個性的なレストランが集中しています。そんな競合店が多く集まるエリアだからこそ、オープンさせたのです。

Chapter 6 **LOCATION**

How to open a coffee shop without avoiding competitors
競合店が集まるエリアに出店する

An area likely to receive media coverage
取材対象になりやすいエリア

It is beneficial to open a coffee shop in an area concentrated with competitors who share the same target customer group who will then tend to frequent the area and share their reviews and information amongst other like-minded people. Additionally, because there are a variety of other coffee shops and restaurants in the surrounding neighborhood, it is easier for the customer as well as the media to go to different places in one visit to the area.

Comparison with competitors brings out the best in your own business.

If you open a shop in an area concentrated with other coffee shops, it is more likely that customers in the area will want to visit new places. It also means that the customer will be able to compare your café with your competitors. Coffee loving customers will tend to visit an area with a selection of coffee shops in the knowledge that even if a certain café is full, there are others to choose from. Again, a highly concentrated area with trendy coffee shops and restaurants, media coverage is more likely. An example would be the "Kiyosumi-Shirakawa" area in Tokyo that is gathering the spotlight.

競合するコーヒー店や個性的な店舗が集中するエリア内には、同じ感度、趣味嗜好をもった対象とするお客様が自然と集まり、口コミで広がりやすい利点があります。また、同じエリア内で簡単に何店舗も回ることができるため、お客様はもちろんのこと、取材する側にも便利なエリアなのです。

お客様に競合店と比べてもらわないと自店のよさが伝わらず、自店の成長もないと考えます。

同じコーヒー店が集中しているエリアに出店していると、そのエリアのお客様は「一度、試してみよう」という気持ちが働き、来店の確率は高くなります。さらにお客様に競合店と自店を比べていただくことができます。また、お客様が目的のコーヒー店がたとえ満席で入店できないと考えても、そのエリア内にほかのコーヒーショップが数店あると安心感が働き、周辺にコーヒー好きのお客様が集まりやすくなります。そして、雑誌の特集記事にも組まれやすいエリアです。現在、東京では、清澄白河のようなところがひとつのエリアとしてあげられます。

Chapter 6 **LOCATION**

Areas to avoid
避けたいエリア

On the other hand, I would not recommend opening a café in a large shopping mall or high-rise complex. It could easily result in an unequal balance of high priced rent yet lack of customer traffic. It is often the case that initially, there is a certain amount of customer traffic due to advertisement and media coverage, however, in the long run, it will depend on how well the entire facility is able to draw customers. Therefore, if you imagine that the facility is the Titanic, individual efforts to keep afloat is practically pointless. There are many examples of famous coffee shops opening satellite shops as a tenant in large complexes, but the reason is purely because the facility management company try to attract well-known tenants in order to benefit from the percentage of sales as part of the rental agreement. However, although it is common for a tenant shop to close, I have yet to see a main flagship shop close while the tenant shop survives.
It is also difficult to recreate the same atmosphere in a tenant shop and it is virtually unheard of that customers prefer a tenant shop over the main shop.In fact, an acquaintance of mine who did not heed to my advice opened a shop in a large commercial facility losing control over any freedom including opening dates and hours, the concept, and ultimately, the staff's motivation.

Never rush the pace of opening new shops

Even amongst customers who are avid fans of your shop, there is always the danger that each time you open a new shop may give the impression that you are going mainstream for profit and will lead to a deterioration in flavor and overall quality.

It is a fact that with every new shop opening, seasoned baristas will be reassigned and their loyal following customers may also leave and inevitably, the quality of the products, services and the rarity will decrease. There are no positive aspects for the loyal customers.

逆に、私が避けたい出店場所は、ショッピングモールや高層ビル内などの大型商業施設のテナント物件と考えています。施設の集客力と家賃が比例していないと最悪の結果になります。大型商業施設の開業時は、広告宣伝して集客がありますが、その後は施設自体の集客にかかってきます。施設がタイタニックのような大型船だと、自分だけ頑張ってもともに沈没する確率は高くなるからです。有名で実績ある店舗が大型商業施設にテナントで支店を出していることがよくありますが、そのほとんどが、売り上げのパーセントが家賃になるため、施設側が有名でより多くの家賃収入が取れそうな店舗を誘致するからです。しかし、支店であるテナント店の撤退は見ても、本店が閉店してテナント店だけ生き残っているのは見たことがありません。テナント店は本店の雰囲気が出しづらく、お客様も本店よりテナント店に愛着をもつことは絶対にありません。事実、私の意見を聞かずに大型商業施設に出店したことで、お店の主導権はなくなり、営業時間や定休日の変更も許されず、さらに施設側の担当者にあれこれ口出しされ、お店の自由、コンセプト、スタッフのやる気さえもなくしたテナント店がありました。

無理ある早い出店ペースは絶対に禁物

いくらお客様がお店の大ファンあっても、お店が急に増えるたびに、「味が落ちるんじゃないか？」「儲けに走った？」など、お客様にチェーン店的な匂いや、悪い印象を与えかねない危険性があります。事実、熟練したバリスタたちが、新店がオープンするたびに分散すると常連客は離れますし、「商品の質・サービス・希少性」は下がっていきます。いまいるリピーターのお客様にとっても、なにもよいことはありません。

Chapter 7
BRANDING

第7章 ブランディング

ブランディングとは、お客様が店を選ぶ基準となるイメージを強化させる戦略のこと。イメージを向上させることで、店（ブランド）に対する信頼感を定着させるのだ。ここでは個人経営のコーヒー店において必要なブランディング要素とはなにか、品質からスタッフ育成まで心がけるべきことを解説する。

Chapter 7 **BRANDING**

Brand philosophy
ブランドの考え方

- Offer a variety of menu in an attempt to target a higher number of customers. Coffee begins to take a second seat.
- Extend opening hours. Increase of staff labor load.
- Expand and wide-spread the business. Becomes just another run of the mill coffee shop.
- Enter a price war with the competitors. An array of drinks and food, etc.... Compared with others leading to an inevitable price - cut – Competition.

- 多彩なドリンク・フードで幅広いメニューを提供 ➡ 本業のコーヒーの存在が薄くなる。
- 営業時間を伸ばす ➡ スタッフのオペレーション労働負荷。
- 不特定多数のマーケットにビジネスを広げる ➡ 一般のお店に成り下がる。
- 競合店と価格で勝負する ➡ 比較されると低価格になり、競争しないといけなくなる。

- Provide an entirely original menu without copying other shops.
- Strive to maximize branding efforts.
- Become a non-competitive establishment through providing a unique service, maintaining differentiation to avoid a price war.
- Intentionally shift your business focus differently from competitors and play the game in your own field.
- Always aim to provide more value than for the price. Target your business to choice clientele.
- Compete for subjective customer satisfaction. Aim for subjective customer satisfaction.

- 他店のマネをしないオリジナルメニューにする。
- 特定な人（マーケット）にビジネスを限定する。
- 独自のサービスを提供して差別化し、非競争な状態をつくることで商品を低価格にさせない。
- ビジネスマーケットを意図的に他社とずらし、自分の土俵だけで戦う。
- ブランド力・価格を上げる状態をつくる。／つねに価格以上の価値の提供を目指す。
- お客様の主観的な満足で勝負する。

Chapter 7　**BRANDING**

Brand strategy for independent coffee shops

個人経営のコーヒーショップが必要な
6つのブランド戦略

1. Always use top quality coffee and milk.
　Never cease to seek improvement.

2. Treasure time and effort and don't just focus on efficiency.
　Become a craftsman and hone skills that no major chain-store or machine can duplicate.

3. Find your passion and originality.
　Never compromise on quality and find a uniqueness.

4. Provide top quality products and service at a reasonable price.
　High quality does not equal high priced that only the affluent can afford. Not tacky.

5. Go above and beyond expectation.
　Seek to provide taste and service surpassing customer expectation.
　Please the customer with a visual presentation exceeding any photographs.

6. Create an original idea.
　Customers will get bored with routine. Come up with new ideas even if they're copied by others.
　Remain open minded and think of it as an honor to be copied.

---

1. 高品質なコーヒーやミルクなどの食材を使用
　つねにおいしさの追求。

2. 効率だけを考えず、手間を惜しまない
　チェーン店や機械ができない高度な技を磨く。職人芸を身につける。

3. 独自のこだわりとオリジナリティ
　妥協をしない商品クオリティとほかにはない仕掛けがある。

4. 誰もが行ける価格帯だが上質
　高級＝富裕層向けの高価格ではなく上質。安っぽくないこと。

5. 期待以上、予想以上
　お客様の期待を越える感動的な味とサービス。メニュー写真や取材写真を越えるビジュアルがある。

6. 他店にないアイデア
　マンネリではお客様に飽きられます。ほかにマネをされても新しいアイデアを生み、
　よいアイデアはマネされるのは当然という広い心をもつこと。

Chapter 7 **BRANDING**

Offer something new and original
体験したことがないものを提供する

The more a shop becomes popular, the more is expected by customers. It then becomes important to rise above the customer's expectation in order to impress them. The higher rated and better reviews there are on internet sources such as Yelp in the US, or Tabelog in Japan, the higher the expectations of the customers as well as a likelihood of harsher criticism from them. Always keep in mind that just one disappointing visit means losing some customers for good.

Do not simply provide what a customer expects. In doing so, there will be no surprises nor new experiences for the customer. What a customer truly seeks is something entirely unexpected and new.

お店が有名になればなるほど、お客様の期待値はどんどん高くなります。お店はその期待通りではなく、期待を越えないとお客様に感動を与えることはできません。いまは、アメリカでは「Yelp」や日本では「食べログ」などレビューの評価が高ければ高いほどお客様の期待値は高くなります。お客様の目は厳しくなります。お客様を一度でも失望させると、二度とリピートしないことを肝に銘じなければいけません。

お客様のニーズにそのまま応えていてはいけません。それではお客様に驚きや感動を与えることはできません。本当のニーズ、お客様の要望とは、お客様が「まだ体験したことがないもの」「飲んだことがないもの」「見たことがないもの」「知らないこと」「これまでになかったもの」にあります。

Chapter 7 **BRANDING**

Focus on a specific target clientele
来ていただきたいお客様に集中する

Aim to become the go-to place for your target clientele rather than trying to reach out to anyone and everyone.

It is impossible to target everyone. The concept becomes unclear in doing so.
The basics of operating a coffee shop and net fishing are similar. With net fishing, it is much wiser to use a large-meshed net in order to capture the big fish. If one becomes greedy and uses a narrow-meshed net in an attempt to capture as many as possible, you run the risk of damaging the big fish while handling the smaller ones. Likewise, losing focus on the target clientele will result in unsatisfied customers, and there is always a chance to widen the target range once the business is stable.

すべての層をターゲットにしてはいけません。もっとも来てほしいお客様層に集中し、オンリーワンの店舗を目指したいものです。

すべての層をターゲットにすることは不可能です。店舗の個性も失います。それは例えると魚の網漁法と同じです。魚を捕る網の目を粗くし、必要な魚のみ捕獲するのです。欲張って網の目を細かくして一網打尽にしようとすると、雑魚の処理に追われて肝心の大物の魚体が傷みます。つまり、肝心のお客様を満足させることはできないのです。店舗も漁法と同じで、それぞれの魚、お客様に合わせた取り方があるのです。

Chapter 7 **BRANDING**

The sole purpose of a business is to serve the customer

商売とは、お客様のためにあります

First and foremost, a shop exists for customers. It is not for any investor, staff member nor for capital gain. One must fully understand that without customers, a shop cannot survive. It would not make sense asking a customer to buy coffee in order to return profits for an investor, or because the staff wish to become rich.

However, there are many shops that remain to have misguided priorities. If a shop focuses on profit and not the customer, it affects the quality of the products and services. Customers will definitely notice. Just as a fish will swim away the moment it notices a lure, customers will also run away upon realizing the greed.

Sales profits will follow by showing sincerity and prioritizing the wish to offer quality products and services to the customer.

お店は、第一にお客様のためにあります。出資者・スタッフのためや、お金儲けのためではありません。お店は、最初にお客様にご来店いただいて成り立っていることをしっかりと理解しなければいけません。「出資者に利益を還元したいからコーヒー買ってください」「スタッフがお金持ちになりたいからコーヒー買ってください」ではおかしい話です。

第一にお客様の笑顔が集まった結果として、スタッフや出資者の幸せやお店に利益がもたらされます。しかし、その順番を間違えたお店が多数存在しています。お店が、お客様ではなく、先にお金儲けだけを見ていると、商品の魅力やサービスにも影響します。それを絶対にお客様は見逃さないのです。魚釣りと同じで、お金儲けという釣り糸が見えた瞬間、その魚が逃げるように、お客様も逃げて行くのです。

お客様のための「素晴らしい商品・サービス」を提供し、どれだけ共感していただいたかで、売上がついてきます。

Chapter 7 **BRANDING**

The target clientele
ターゲットにしたい層

A refined and sophisticated clientele. Possessing a sense of fashion and is a gourmet.
People who recognize and appreciate the real thing, willing to pay for quality.
⇨ **The best coffee shop interior is the customer**

ファン客層

感度、センスのよい客層。ファッションセンスもよくおしゃれでグルメ。上質なものにきちんとお金を払う、本物を知っている層。
➡ お店にとって最高のインテリアは、来店しているお客様です。

Non-target customer clientele
ターゲットにしたくない層

Customers who only visit a shop because it is new. Follows a common trend.
⇨ **In other words, not a loyal clientele. Once the trend blows over, the shop will be empty.**

Non-gourmet customers who tend to choose price over quality.
⇨ **It is impossible for independent coffee shops to get ahead in a price cutting competition. This type of customer will simply flow towards a cheaper shop. Nothing can be really cheap yet tasty and safe. There is always a standard price for value.**

浮遊客層

新しいお店がオープンすると、そのお店に流れる、新しいもの好き。流行に流されるミーハー層。
➡ リピーターになってくれない層。流行が終わるとお店は閑古鳥になります。

もともとグルメではない、安い価格に流れる客層

➡ 個人店で価格競争は無理。さらに安いお店を見つけるとそのお店に流れます。激安で本当においしく安全なものはありません。適正価格がきちんとあります。

Chapter 7 **BRANDING**

The branding pyramid
顧客ブランディングピラミッド

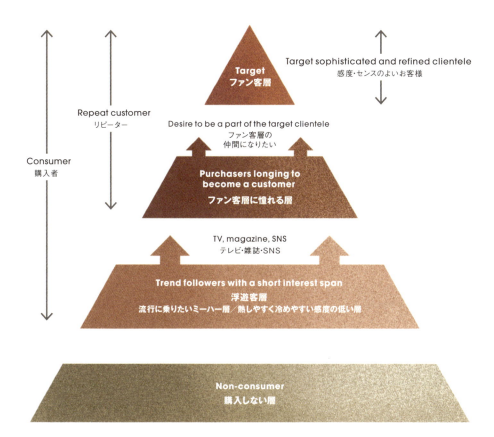

The initial weeks after an opening, it is likely that the majority of the customers will not be your target clientele, therefore it may take some time for the branding and concept to sink in. However, this method allows one to create a long-lasting, impressionable brand.
On the other hand, a shop targeting the less desirable clientele is bound to follow the road to a steady decline after being caught up in a price-cutting war. Without being able to attract repeat customers, the glory days of the first few weeks will not last.

オープン時など最初対象とする客層は絶対数が少ない。よってブランド浸透に時間がかかるが、長く続く強いブランドが形成されていく。最初から感度が低い客層を対象にすると、リピーターにならずに価格競争の道をたどり、息が短いブランドになる。例としては最初だけ行列をつくっていたが、後で閑古鳥の店がそれである。

Chapter 7 **BRANDING**

The staff should be a part of the brand
スタッフにもブランディングは必要

Branding not only exists for the customers. Shop staff should also be a part of the brand.

I love working here.
I learn something new everyday.
I'm given responsibility.
I'm given a fair review and efforts appreciated.
I can experience personal growth.
My colleagues are professionals and the customers are great.
I would visit this shop everyday as a customer.
My workplace is somewhere I can brag about to my family and friends.

ブランディングは、お客様に対してだけではいけません。お店で働くスタッフ全員に対してもブランディングが必要です。

「ここで働くことが楽しい」
「日々、勉強になる」
「任せてもらえる」
「評価してもらえる」
「自分自身が成長できる」
「一緒に働くスタッフのレベルは高く客層もよい」
「自分も毎日でもお客様として来たいお店」
「家族や友人に自慢できるお店」など。

上記のように思うような働く場をつくることが重要です。

Chapter 8
BARISTA

第 8 章　バリスタ

著者自身もバリスタという目線でコーヒーショップを成功に導いているようにコーヒーショップにおいて、バリスタは欠かせない存在だ。店では職人バリスタはどういう存在であるべきなのか。単に技術が高くてもいけない、さらに言えばホスピタリティだけではいけない。日々の生活を鍛錬することがすべてに繋がっていく。そして、もちろん経営者もバリスタのやる気を支えることも大事なのだ。

Chapter 8 **BARISTA**

The ideal barista
理想のバリスタ像

Hospitality, modesty and kindness are traits that every person should possess. One should always act cordially to everyone, be that colleagues or customers, and always remain compassionate and thankful. In Japan, there is an old proverb "the boughs that bear most hang lowest". Just as the more fruit it bears the lower the bough hangs, the more a person becomes enlightened, the more modest and humble one becomes. On the other hand, the more boastful a lesser person is. It is important to carefully choose staff who befit the shop's concept as well as is compatible with the target clientele.

Early to bed, early to rise
Personal healthcare management is a must and a barista should not stay up late only to greet customers in the morning with a sleepy face.

A barista should be gourmet with no likes and dislikes
Without a genuine interest in food, developing new menu ideas are slim and one is unable to provide the best service. Personally experience and taste all types of cuisine from top to bottom. To possess the curiosity and to perceive money spent for food as a personal investment is important.

A barista should be hip, neat with a good sense of fashion.
Stylish customers will not visit a coffee shop with poor taste. Fashion is a frequent topic in conversation with the customers. A sloppy person cannot work at a decent coffee shop.

Non-smoker
Smoking cigarettes harms the sense of smell and taste. A barista needs a honed sense of smell and taste, therefore, I would recommend smokers to quit smoking and use that money for self investment.

Slim silhouette
A barista's job entails long hours on one's feet. Being overweight is not only unhealthy but also damages knees in order to support the extra weight. Customers tend not to buy sweets such as doughnuts and cookies if recommended from an overweight barista. They would think whether the sweets are high in calories and by eating them, they may also gain weight.It is a given fact that there is a correlation between the sales figures of sweets and the appearance of the seller. Statistics show that overweight people are less likely to be hired in sweets and chocolate shops in Japan (depending on the obesity).

Loves to study and loves to talk
In order to come up with new ideas, not only should a barista be well read, well versed and knowledgeable in coffee, but a variety of topics. Without knowledge and information, one can only hold superficial conversations and interactions with the customers.

Be ambitious and welcome new challenges
Remember that there is always someone better. One cannot mature living in a state of constant fear of failure. One cannot gain stability by remaining listless and indifferent. Opportunities await where the majority, in fear of failure, do not venture. Participating in the barista world championship competition is an excellent platform to compete with others from around the world and to measure your technical skills.

A professional barista must possess a high level of expertise knowledge and skill, and is able to control emotions, remains logical and always puts the customer first.

Chapter 8 **BARISTA**

いくらよい商品やスタッフに技術、能力があっても、スタッフのヤル気、モチベーションが低いと成果は上がりません。人として、ホスピタリティは当然のことです。一緒に働く仲間やお客様、すべての人に対して、思いやり、心からのおもてなし、感謝の気持ちをつねに持つこと。日本には、「実るほど頭を垂れる稲穂かな」という言葉があります。稲が実を熟すほど穂が垂れ下がるように、人間も学問や徳が深まるにつれ謙虚になり、小人物ほど、高ぶって偉そうにふるまうもの。お店のコンセプトにふさわしく、ターゲットにしたお客様の対応ができる人材を妥協せず採用しなければいけません。ここでは理想のバリスタ像を7つあげます。もちろん、これにあてはめる必要はありませんが、真のサービスとはなにかと求めると、こうなるのです。

早寝早起き
健康管理は当然のこと、夜更かしして朝に眠そうな顔でお客様を迎えることはできません。

食べ物の好き嫌いがなく、グルメ
食に対して興味がないと、新しいメニューのアイデアも出ませんし、素晴らしいサービスもできません。世界の食材から高級レストランまで、自分の目と舌で確認する。自分投資のため、食にお金を使う、あくなき好奇心が必要です。

オシャレで、清潔。センスがよい
趣味が悪いところにお洒落なお客様は来ません。お客様とファッションの話もしたい。清潔感がないと飲食店で働くのは無理です。

非喫煙者
喫煙すると、臭覚・味覚の感覚が鈍る。バリスタには研ぎ澄まされた臭覚と味覚が必要です。タバコ代を自分投資に使ったほうがよいと考えます。

体型がスマート
バリスタは長時間の立ち仕事。肥満は自分の体重を支えるのに膝に負担がかかり悪くする。健康のためにも痩せたほうがよい。
太ったバリスタが、コーヒーのおともで、ドーナツやクッキーなどのスイーツをお客様にオススメしても買ってもらえません。「この店のスイーツはカロリーが高い？」「食べるとこんな体型に？」と思われてしまいます。事実、店員の見た目でスイーツの売上は変わるので、日本のスイーツショップやチョコレート店などでは太っている人を採用しないことが多いという統計があります（ただし肥満度合によります）。

学び好き・会話好き
コーヒーのことだけではなく、いろいろなことを勉強し、いろいろな人と会話して、体験してアイデアが出ます。自分に情報量が少ないと、いろいろなお客様と中身のある会話ができません。

向上心がありチャレンジ精神がある
上には上がいると思うこと。失敗を恐れ、挑戦しない人には成長はありません。なにもやらない安定志向に魅力もなければ安定もありません。多くの人が失敗を恐れて手をつけていないところにチャンスがあります。バリスタのチャンピオンシップに出場し、世界と戦い、自分の技術のレベルを確認するのもよいと思います。

プロのバリスタとは、高い専門知識と高度な技術をもち、感情をコントロールし、理性で行動出来る、顧客第一主義の人です。

Chapter 8 **BARISTA**

The Barista Championship
バリスタのチャンピオンシップについて

I think that both participants and the event staff should understand that the Barista Championship is a performing entertainment. Without an audience and communicativity, there is no meaning to the event. Unless the event is held on "holy ground" such as Las Vegas is to boxing and Seattle is to barista competitions, in the same sense as operating a coffee shop, there is a dire need to meticulously plan and include an entertainment factor in order to bring in an audience. Equally important is to produce a "star barista" from these events in order to bring in high leveled baristas to participate and compete. Unfortunately, there are championship events held all over the world featuring mediocre participants and a decreasing number of a disinterested audience.

A number of barista champions have asked me why they're not famous even if they have won. It is mutually the fault of the event sponsors as well as the participating baristas who simply want to "win". As is the case with professional sports, it is only natural that fans lose interest if the game is always boring. A participant should envision how to entertain the audience, give a unique and original performance, and how to impress the judges. The barista needs to consider the most effective method of how to differentiate oneself from the competition as well as personal branding.

Luckily, I was blessed in both timing and venue when I won the 2008 championship which was not only held in Seattle, but also prior to the Lehmann shock when there was more hype about the event. Even so, my foremost efforts were spent in trying to figure out how to entertain the audience and judges with a brand new latte art form and stunning performance.

バリスタのチャンピオンシップは、開催する側も出場するバリスタ側も「興行」だということを理解しなければいけないと思います。より多くの観客を集め、発信力がないと開催する意味がありません。店舗経営と同じく開催する側は、バリスタの大会だとシアトル、ボクシングだとラスベガスのような聖地、一等地で大きく開催し、さらに、観客（お客様）をいかに集客する仕掛けを考えないと思います。また、そこからスターバリスタを輩出し、スターを目指すレベルの高い出場者を増やすことも考えることが必要です。現在、残念ながらマンネリで観客数も伸びず、出場者のレベルも低い発信力のないチャンピオンシップが各地で開催されています。

何人かのバリスタから「なぜ優勝しても自分の知名度がなぜ上がらないか」と聞かれたことがあります。開催する側の責任もありますが、出場するバリスタ側も、単に勝ちにこだわっていているだけではいけません。プロスポーツと同じく、つまらないプレーだけをしていると、ファンがいなくなるのです。いかに観客を喜ばすパフォーマンスをするか、ほかの出場者との明らかな違いや、インパクトを審査員に与えることを考えて出場しなくてはいけません。自分自身の差別化とＰＲ、ブランディングが必要です。

私が優勝した2008年の大会は、リーマンショック前で大会自体がいまよりも盛り上がっていましたし、シアトルで優勝したという、時代的、場所的にも恵まれていたこともありますが、私はいままで誰もやっていないラテアートやパフォーマンスして、観客と審査員を楽しませることに全力を尽くしました。

WORLD COFFEE Battle
Latte Art

Hiroshi Sawada

- 2015 Produced the HARIO x Hiroshi Sawada Free Pour Latte Art Pitcher worldwide
- 2012 Honored as one of "Japanese who have reached the top of the world" in Newsweek Japan
- 2011 Became the first Asian to appear on the cover of Barista Magazine, published in the US
- 2010 Opened Streamer Coffee Company in Shibuya, Tokyo
- 2009 Published the world's first technical book on free pou[r]
- 2008 First Asian winner of Latte Art World Championship in Seattle, USA, with a record-breaking high score

정경우

- 2015 WLAC 월드라떼아트챔피언쉽 3위
- 2015 WBC 국가대표 선발전 바리스타부문 8위

Chapter 8 BARISTA

Barista requirements to demonstrate the skills at the championship

チャンピオンシップで実力が発揮できる
バリスタの条件

Chapter 8 **BARISTA**

Preparation is key.
Practice longer than your competitors. Handling equipment and tools you are unfamiliar with brings a feeling of insecurity. Practice and familiarize yourself with the actual machine used at the event and bring your own tools and dress comfortably. Being prepared is key to confidence.

Arrive early.
It is best to be the first one there to get accustomed to the atmosphere before the crowd. Being surrounded by strangers can also be unnerving so try to hold conversations with as many people as possible to relax.

Do what you do best and don't focus on winning.
Just give your best performance for the audience and judges as you would do for customers who visit your coffee shop. Refrain from trying something you are unaccustomed to and entirely new as it will only make you nervous.

Do not watch your competitors performance.
Watching or hearing a competitor's positive performance results will put extra pressure on you to outperform them. Simply do the best you can and focus on competing with yourself.

Health management.
No one is able to perform well in bad health conditions. As well as daily health management and a healthy diet, the consumption of food and drink prior to a competition is important. Lack of calcium and magnesium can cause anxiety, over excitement and shivers so it is recommended that you supplement your diet with vitamin and minerals before a major event. Personally, I always kept a Clif Bar with me so that I was neither full nor hungry during the event.

事前準備は必要
自分より練習量が多い選手はいないと断言できるほど練習する。触ったことがない、マシーンや器具は不安が生まれるもの。事前にチャンピオンシップで使用するマシーンで納得できるまで練習し、普段使用している器具、さらには身につける腕時計や靴なども持参する。準備ができていると自信にもつながる。

会場入りは1番
会場の雰囲気に飲まれないよう、誰よりも早く会場に到着し、場慣れしておくことが大切。チャンスがあれば、審査員や他の選手と会話する。周りが初対面ばかりでは、過度の緊張を生むので、リラックスするためにも、初対面の人とできる限り会話をする。

勝ちにこだわり過ぎず、いつもの自分がやっている仕事をする
普段、お店でお客様を楽しませていることを、観客・審査員の前でやればよい。普段まったくやっていないことは"アガリ"を生む。

ほかの選手の競技やラテアートは見ない
自分より前の他選手の競技がうまくできているのを見たり聞いたりすると、自分の順番が来たときに余計な力が入り過ぎる。いまの自分の実力だけ出せばよい。自分に勝つことだけに集中する。

健康管理
体調が悪いと実力が発揮できない。普段からの健康管理はもちろんのこと、食事の栄養バランス、競技前の食事や飲み物は大切。カルシウムやマグネシウムが不足すると、興奮や体の震え、不安感が大きくなる場合があるので、緊張感がある大会には必要なビタミン・ミネラルは補給する。ちなみに私は、競技直前は、お腹がいっぱいでも空いていてもいけないので、つねに「クリフバー」を携帯していた。

澤田洋史　Hiroshi Sawada

Sawada coffeeオーナーバリスタ。大阪府出身。近畿大学商経学部経営学科卒業。2008年米国シアトルで開催された「Latte Art World Championship」にて歴代最高スコアでアジア人初の世界チャンピオンとなる。2009年、世界で初、Free pour Latte Artの専門書を出版。2010年、東京・渋谷に「STREAMER COFFEE COMPANY」をオープン。テレビ番組「世界を変える100人の日本人」に出演や2001年には世界でもっとも権威あるコーヒー専門誌『バリスタマガジン』(米国発行)ではアジア人初の表紙を飾る。また、『ニューズウィーク』誌の「世界の頂点を極めた日本人」に選出。Mercedes-Benz Connectionのカフェ、DOWNSTAIRS COFFEEをプロデュース。2015年、「STREAMER COFFEE COMPANY」を退任後、シカゴに「sawada coffee USA」をオープン。www.sawadacoffee.com

Owner/Barista of Sawada coffee, Chicago, USA. www.sawadacoffee.com
Hometown: Osaka, Japan. Graduated from Kindai University, faculty of commerce and economics. Became the first Asian World Champion Barista of "Latte Art World Championship" held in Seattle with recording the highest score in history. Published the world first Free pour Latte Art book in 2009. Opened "STREAMER COFFEE COMPANY" in Shibuya, Tokyo in 2010. Appeared in TV program "100 Japanese people who change the world" in 2010. Be the first Asian Barista on the cover of most famous coffee specialized magazine "Barista Magazine" published in 2011. Produced DOWNSTAIRS COFFEE of Mercedes-Benz Connection in 2011. Selected as "A Japanese person who has achieved the summit of the world" in "Newsweek" published in 2012. Quit "STREAMER COFFEE COMPANY" and opened "sawada coffee" in Chicago, USA in 2015.

写真
Kevin J. Miyazaki
[P14-15, 18-19, 22, 23, 26-27, 29, 38-39, 48, 52, 56-57, 58, 67, 68, 74-75, 78, 80-81, 84, 86-87, 90-91, 94-95, 98-99, 100-101, 102-103, 106-107, 108, 111, 114-115, 122, 125, 131, 136-137]

Akiko Arai (SOSOUP) [P64, 72, 76, 96]

Hiroshi Sawada

翻訳・英文ネイティブチェック
Yukiko Ishimaru
Takahiro Maekawa

デザイン
Yoshihiro Kato (OFFIBA DESIGN)

編集協力
Rachel Gillman Rischall (HOGSALT)
Jean Tomaro (HOGSALT)

編集
Fuyuko Kita

sawada coffee style
バリスタ澤田洋史に学ぶコーヒーショップのつくりかた

2016年10月9日　初版第1刷発行

著者：澤田 洋史

発行：トランスワールドジャパン株式会社
〒150-0001 東京都渋谷区神宮前6-34-15 モンターナビル
Tel: 03-5778-8599　Fax:03-5778-8743
発行人：佐野 裕

印刷・製本：中央精版印刷株式会社

Printed in Japan
©Hiroshi Sawada, Transworld Japan Inc. 2016

定価はカバーに表示されています。
本書の全部または一部を、著作権法で認められた範囲を超えて無断で複写、複製、あるいはデジタル化する事を禁じます。
乱丁・落丁本は小社送料負担にてお取り替え致します。

ISBN 978-4-86256-187-9